TELL

Soraya Peerbaye

# Tell
poems for a girlhood

PEDLAR PRESS | St. John's

For information, write Pedlar Press at
113 Bond Street, St John's NL A1C 1T6 Canada

COVER ART Karine Guyon, *There is Light*
DESIGN Oberholtzer Design Inc., St John's NL
TYPEFACES Garamond, Allise

PRINTED IN CANADA
Coach House Printing

LIBRARY AND ARCHIVES CANADA CATALOGUING IN PUBLICATION
Peerbaye, Soraya, 1971–, author
     Tell : poems for a girlhood / Soraya Peerbaye.

Poems.

ISBN 978-1-897141-72-4 (paperback)
     1. Virk, Reena, 1983-1997 — Poetry.  1. Title.

PS8631.E395T45 2015       C811'.6       C2015-904769-2

ACKNOWLEDGEMENTS
The publisher wishes to thank the Canada Council for the Arts and the NL Publishers Assistance Program for their generous support of our publishing program.

*for Sheila*

# CONTENTS

## TELL

## THE LANDSCAPE WITHOUT HER

# Trials

Magnolias in bloom, each trial held in early spring.
Pink-white curve of petals like skinned knees.
Newspapers opened to her eighth grade photograph:
black curls, bronze smile, heirloom gold earring.

In the courtroom, articles of clothing suggested her.
*Exhibits.* Out of the pleather jacket her torso emerged;
out of her clog boots, her stance. She believed in this,
that her body could be enough. As a girl, I would have liked
to be like that, to have her daring. Still – hard to say,
if I'd have been her friend – her ardour, pungent, dangerous.

*Even flowers are ranked,* said the woman watching
the proceedings with me. *Roses are worth more
than daisies. Lilies more than daffodils.* I want
her body to stand, be its own testimony. Instead
it's the jacket, held before the witness,

        open, declarative,

while the fair-haired girl behind Plexiglas
says nothing.

SEARCH

# Rainfall

To be sure of nothing
but moon waning gibbous. Her body
in the Gorge, drifting.

Dewpoint. Night wind blowing
seven kilometres per hour. *That the water
would have been near 9.9° Celsius . . .*

*. . . That there was no rain in Victoria on November 14th, 1997,*
          *but that*
*it rained several days between then and the 22nd . . .*

Eight nights. To be sure of nothing
but rainfall, careful
measurements. The tenth of a millimetre. Notations
of absence. *Trace, nil.*

# Tide

Would I have seen her?

The tide tugging her gently past
the Comfort Inn; houses, tall and gabled,
the bridge and its passersby.
This is not a hidden place.

The graze and drag of her,
clumsy, obstructive in the divided
caress of eelgrass.

No search. Eight days.
Nights,
the moon returned, made chalk tracings around her shape.

# Silt

The Gorge, thick and brown
with sewage, run-off. Rainwater

carrying copper, zinc, mercury,
hydrocarbons in the storm drain. Contaminants
in the watershed.

Wood debris from decades
of sawmill and log boom operations
by the Selkirk Bridge.

*. . . silt, shells, bottles, trash, eelgrass . . .*

Drifts of anoxic water. Sediment, *heavy,* clogging
the gills of fish.

# Current

Her jeans, knotted around her ankles,
coming undone,

unbodied.

*Her garments . . . saturated . . . soiled . . .*

They read currents by the constellation
of their findings. *A light covering of silt*
in the folds of her clothing. Ribbons of eelgrass,
*green on one side, silt-laden*
*on the other.*

# Reena

*She could have been a girl, a boy, a fish,*
*whatever –*

Warren said –
the night of his arrest, her body not yet found.

# Silt

She sways, shifts,
a hunch the current follows.

Chagrined, it sifts the shirt,
the camisole, the effortless hair.
(Earring tangled there, gold crustacean.)

She is a slow, sunken spin, slow sweep below. Silt-
stroked eyes. Silt-stroked tongue. The inlet of her
mouth, silt-stroked teeth.

# Willow

In the aerial, deep greens give way
to blues, brown
and cream of shallows.
Like the cloud-and-wind paintings we made
in Grade five, the year we studied Persia:
ink and turpentine floated on water, whorled,
before we laid the blank sheet of paper
down.

> *– Where the yellow tree is, there?*

*– Yes.*

> *– And we're to look below*
> *to that small, darker object?*

> > *– Yes, mm-hm.*

# Saanich

Quarter moon high in the sky at dawn.
The Gorge in flood tide.

*Saanich,* a Salish word, saline
language in the mouth: to emerge,
as from water.

> *. . . what a child might call*
> *a jellyfish position,*

rounded shoulders, arms and legs draping downwards
in the shallows.

> *. . . in a small cove,* said the diver,
*where there is little movement, so things*
*gather.*

November leaves, trash, hair
snagged in the reeds.

The sluggish current turning and returning,
obsessive.

# Admission of Facts

*That the body of Reena Virk was transported to Victoria General*
*Hospital in the City of Victoria, British Columbia, where Dr. Laurel*
*Gray, a forensic pathologist, conducted the autopsy on the body,*
*November 24th, 1997.*

# Washerwoman

The pathologist separated injury
from *immersion change,*

*the wrinkly 'washerwoman' appearance*
of palms and soles.

I thought of the brown-skinned washerwomen, back on the island,
standing up to their thighs in water, in saris.
Slap of clothes, bubbles streaming downriver
along bright-coloured palus;
grey soap scum at the edge.

She spoke of surface layers
slackened, sloughed –

    *skin slippage,*

the body bloated, firm to the touch,

*tense.*

# Autopsy

I.

      The way certain things could be hidden

by darker skin, the heaviness of hair
        on the body.

    *Immersion too*

          *makes surface bruises*
      *more difficult to see.*

2.

The smallest injuries, first:

        *chatter marks*
     *fingernails crossing*

           *scraping up*

*little bits of skin*

            *then skipping down.*

3.

      A burn mark between the eyebrows

the ulcerated

          punched-out shape

    *consistent*

       *with a cigarette.*

4.

      *Bloody discharge from the nose . . .*
*bruised cheek, bruised*

              *mouth and chin, dark red*

*bruising about her lips . . .*

      *Fine bruises*
on back         flanks        abdomen;

                *pinkish, pinky-orange bruises*
         *symmetrical on both shoulders*

            *which might represent*       *grip marks.*

      *Bruising, deep*
*into the soft tissue of the face . . . bruising*

            *down to the skull bone, yes.*

A word like sediment, layer
      upon layer. Blood

             slowed, sullen

                  stilled.

     The colours in the photographs so mottled
the Crown asked

          *Are these colours true?*

5.

    The head, when shaven:

*. . . a textured pattern . . .*

        *suggestive of the sole of a running shoe . . .*

6.

    The pathologist's hands, along

the throat's interior

        the tongue, the bone below.


    Hands moving in the mouth.

        A woman's hands. A girl's mouth.

Hands. Force. Law. At times she spoke of Reena

        as she might

    someone she knew, someone living.

        *A healthy young woman,* she said.

    Other times she spoke as though the body

could say what it wanted.

        *There are different kinds of shock*

        *but I think in her case it would be a desire*
        *to save herself.*

# À PLEINE GORGE

*Testimony of Warren Glowatski*
*R. v. Kelly Marie Ellard, 2004*

# Gorge Waterway

The word that in my mother tongue means throat –
   *gorge* – here,

a glacier-carved passage; the sea, brash,
moving inland, toward

the shirred surrender of the estuary.

Salt marshes; mudflats at the mouths of Craigflower Creek,
Colquitz River; eelgrass meadows.

Throat, and the breasts of birds – *rouge-gorge, oiseau-mouche
à gorge rubis, moqueur gorge-blanche.*

There had been the tumult of rumour, trials, an overturned
verdict, then silence. A shoaling.

*We could tell by her breathing,* said Warren. So they
knelt by her body, then. Listened.

~

He testified how her jeans slid from her hips as they dragged her
face-down to the water. Hair darkening

the breadth of her back, her buttocks, the backs of her legs.
Black-grassed meadow.

*Faire des gorges chaudes de quelque chose, de quelqu'un,*
to laugh at something or someone.

Amidst exotic blackberry, thickets of snowberry and Nootka rose:
clusters of white drupes, luminescent, ceremonial;

crimson rosehips on red-thorned stems, blackening
in late fall.

~

He refused to testify at Kelly's first trial.
Contempt of court. The stuttered drift of tides.

– *What happened then?*
        – *She started mumbling words.*

Seven years later, he gives us a moment
from the water's edge. An in-between place.

Wanting something to catch those words, wanting
the little lives

that gather what they can by feel.
Feather, fan, siphon; filament and spine.

*Is this possible?* the Crown asked the pathologist. She spoke
of the scalp, *soft and boggy.*

The brain, delicate coral of self. The swelling
cortex. Seizure, speech.

~

In Warren's telling, she drowns looking up, so that she sees
her assailant through water. Face

blurred, but the hands
clear.

Two girls. One standing, water up to her pelvis. The other
supine, her feet trying to find purchase.

He stood on the shore, he said; saw Kelly raise her arm
then bring it down.

*Open hand*, the edge of her palm.

The pathologist followed the descent of bruise
almost to bone. *The hyoid.* An archaeology of throat.

*Son refus m'est resté dans la gorge,* her refusal
stuck in my craw.

Oysters, shells marking the periphery of their silence. Year
after year. Rough grey rings of secretions without; within,

smooth ligament scars.

~

In that other telling, the one that must be true, her face
pressed to the estuary floor.

Sand and pebbles, crushed shells. Brackish water. It floods
her mouth, her nostrils.

Exhibit 18, the envelope of small stones taken from her throat.
*A teaspoon,* said the pathologist. As though speaking

of sugar, salt.

Saltwater, sweetwater, a whirlpool. *Je lui enfoncerai
les mots dans la gorge,* I'll make her eat her words.

Moon on water, pearl and black.
*Red glaze.*

How could he see? *From the moonlight
glimmering on the water.*

~

(In the half-light of the museum, the Aboriginal fishing tool
in its glass case.

*The fish swallows the baited gorge, then tries to spit it out.*
*The gorge*

*turns, wedging in the throat of the fish . . . )*

~

I walk with the word in my mouth, because of the cause
of death: not

the skin layer, fatty layer, muscle layer, *sheared*
from each other; not the organs

crushed against the backbone; not
the trauma to the brain.

*The cause of death was drowning.*

His clothes crumpled in the washing machine's
silver drum, the thrum of water.

*Go check Kelly's jacket,* said Warren. *She said her jacket*
*reeked, like blood, like rotten fish.*

# À pleine gorge

As though they wanted to gorge her most of all.
*You're pointing here, to your throat,*
*to your Adam's apple?* the Crown asked Warren.

Throated, having a throat of a specified characteristic. *Bruant*
*à gorge noire,* black-throated sparrow,
> *gorgebleue à miroir,* bluethroat flycatcher.

*Rire, pleurer, chanter à pleine gorge.* Full-throated laughter, cry,
song.

# Hyoid

*The horseshoe-shaped bone*
*in the throat.*

      Tongue-bone.

Her throat opened,
to see the bruise
stain, sink

down through skin, tissue.

*. . . the edge of the hand*
*brought down like a hatchet blow . . .*

      *I don't want to hear this,* said Warren,
as though he hadn't seen it. As though
the elements returned, involuntary:
yawned: hyoid, hair.

Tongue goes
that deep, turns
at the faintest pressure
against soft palate.
Tongue touching something that won't come,
that retches and won't come,
that won't get used to being touched.
That twists. The tongue in the way of itself.

# Slow time

Maybe it's geologies I love. I am
nine, in a ravine,
its origins in mind

like a dream:
a red river, volcanic, black-
crusted and thick. Holds of basaltic
rock for my hands, I clamber
with my father, my brother
in the Gorges de la Rivière Noire.

Here the force is ice: the receding tongue
of the glacier causing the land to lift,
leaving it isolated from the influence of tides.

A series of shallow lakes,
a swamp surrounded by forest.

The stratum of peat is the story:
litter of pine cones holding themselves
close, their hard brown petals. To be a child,
to be overwhelmed by slow time, event
of ten thousand years,
the violent rush of tides without witness. The ocean
rising again, wanting the Gorge.

Once I dreamed huge trees at the edge of a sea
that is no longer there. Roots unearthed,
carved out, like old teeth. Salt lines
on tree trunks.

# Stones

I will take anything
that is given

the gleam of her mouth

black-throated, bluethroat

froth like frog spawn, or
moons upon moons

forceps descending
to lift pebbles from a girl's throat.

> *– What do the pebbles tell you?*

*– That she was alive when taken into the water;*
*that she was pressed face-down in the Gorge,*

that it became
harder
that she had to be more brave

the quick coil and suck,
turmoil

within,

watery night against her open eyes.

This is what we use for tenderness

the terminology we are given:
*agonal gasp,*
clutch of tongue between the teeth

the common gestures of the drowned, the common gifts
they bring when we dredge them back. *A reed clutched in the hand.*

# Tendre la gorge

Three girls walked together the next morning.

> *– We went across the Craigflower Bridge,*
> *all the way down the waterway.*

> *– Why?*

> *– Kelly wanted us to walk along the Gorge to see*
> *if we could find any of her clothes . . .*

> *. . . We stopped at Tillicum Bridge . . .*

*. . . Kelly said she smashed her head into a tree . . . Kelly said*
*they dragged her to the water's edge . . . Kelly said*
*Reena's jeans came off, and she stopped and filled them with rocks*
*and tied them around her ankles. Kelly*
*was angry at Warren because he wouldn't help her . . .*
*Kelly said she held Reena's head under*
*while she had a smoke . . .*

~

*Tendre la gorge.* To surrender, but it's the word *tendre*
I want – I wish her that, some tenderness

to undo what was done.

# WHO YOU WERE

# Lagoons and lakes

There was the sea, yes; blue held
between the island and its hem of coral.
I liked diving best, the warm, lemony
taste of seawater, the fizz of sand
like leaning my ear to the rim of a glass of Fanta.
Afterwards, salt crusted my eyelashes, cracked
my lips; I sat in the sun with my arms wrapped round
my legs, licked the fine, bitter dust on the insides
of wrists, elbows, the tops of knees.

Here it was sweet water, sweet stones;
the pebble-click language of lakes.

Always stepping in to be carried: to be
lifted, tilted and tear-dropped, set down
by swells on toe-tips. To be swayed. Whole afternoons
spent like this; at the end of the day I would lie in bed,
    feeling water,
turbulent ghost moving through me, my body
not yet accustomed to the bed's smooth,
rippled beach.

# Chemistry

I was the girl watching
my science teacher, the demonstration
of the classroom experiment,
burning a hard ribbon in a crucible
to make magnesium oxide.

I could feel the strangeness of standing inside a body
looking out:
could hear my eyelids open and close with a click
as though lids were bone.
Breathing, open-mouthed, I let
the stream of air pass between
teeth, over tip of tongue, to throat.
I felt as though I were standing in a doorway
to myself, decoding
how to enter.

Even now, the memory of that experiment comes back:
blackboards, gleaming sinks; my fingers twisting
the burner's ring to intensify the flow of gas.
I held the metal to the three blue flames, one inside the other,
to the innermost one. Then the white
flare, blue flame becoming
gold,

how for a moment I stepped
into wonder, a clearing
without threshold, full of breath.

# Beauty

Scar-shine of knees,
spine, scoliosed with shy.
Seahorse spine. *Could she
come out of her shell?*
Home, I locked my door, stood
against the wall, naked,
slid a hand into small
of back. Pressed spine
toward knuckles. Jutting
hipbone, sacrum, black-mounded
pubis, parts of the body I hated
for being sex when nothing of me
could be wanted.

Looked in the mirror
to the girl there, grey-green-
tinged, emerald only
in the bevelled edge. Turned
the pages of my beauty books
to learn how to have
a back like theirs, skin
like theirs, eyes. That one
in lotus pose, spine
the imprint a rivulet
leaves. That one
with her morning ritual,

thin circlets of cucumber
over her eyes,
so lucent I could see
her closed eyelids
beneath milky green.

# Nothing, nothing,

I answered, when my mother asked what happened.

Girls encircling me, chiming as they queried
the beauty traits of the women
of "my country." Elusive
silver smiles, shifting
from face to face,
too close.

Boys' teeth-kisses,
yips and howls in hallways;
the way they punched
their hips, amber stream from juice boxes
between their legs as I passed by.

At the school dance,
I wallflowered
in my lace-ruffled dress, my good shoes,
watched them move,
eyes closed, strobed and juddered
in the magenta-flooded gymnasium.

No valentines.
The *ugh*
of the side left with me
in games of murder ball.

Coming home
and undressing, observing
little bruises, the shape and colour
of sea urchins; remembering

how my brother and I held them,
their delicate, prickly walk across our palms.

# Skin

It wasn't said. What we were, beneath the skin of our respectability.
My father, a doctor, his accent learned from Indians who studied
in England. My mother, a Mary Kay consultant: pink makeup kits
in the living room, the paperback success story on her night table.
How I dreamed of her winning the pink fur-trimmed coat,
the pink Cadillac.

Unsaid, as she held my brother's hand, going door to door to find
out who had beaten him with a bag full of bottles. Her wrist
a golden ribbon between the gap of coat sleeve and glove.

~

Once, I woke in the morning and looked out my window to see
boot prints in fresh snow. A trampled path, as though someone had
taken a shortcut through our backyard, suddenly unsure which way
to go. As though I'd rubbed my eyes too hard, opened them again
to see dark stains on the light. An afterimage. The watermark
on my grandfather's stationery.

I went outside in my nightgown and winter boots. Stomped it
out, beat my arms, did a little chicken dance of fury and shame.
*Paki.* I wasn't even – A word, mouthed in snow.

~

I perfected my English. That is not what I am. I wasn't even from there, didn't speak that language, was not dark brown like the servants, *les bonnes* who cleaned our house, the chauffeur, the gardener, the tailor "back home." Bhai Aziz, Bhai Yousouf, Shiva. Did not carry the bitter scent of turmeric on my skin, the smoky rose of agarbhatti; did not glisten with the shine of almond oil and sweat. That is not what I am. That is not what I am. I perfected my English.

# Safety

Amidst hotel sewing kits, bobby pins, buttons; rupee coins and suitcase keys; razor heads and makeup compacts like mermaids' purses. Little things. I locked myself in the bathroom, moved my hands through cabinet drawers looking for my mother's medications, my father's pharmaceutical samples, the ones for pain, depression, sleep.

Capsules with their cake sprinkle interiors, tablets that left their bitter stardust on my tongue. I waited for the hallucination, put on Nick Kershaw's *Wouldn't It Be Good* and daydreamed the daydream, the one where I was running, slow bass pulse the soundtrack for the chase, trickle like a thumb piano or a river, swell of synth when the sky hatch opened and the aliens abducted me to safety.

What was it I wanted? Not suicide, no. I woke up and there was love, love in silver foil blister packs and cellophane, my mother crying, her face blurred like a moon over water.

~

Then my parents speaking in low voices, my mother exclaiming in a whimper. *Viral meningitis.* Oh eye roll and flutter, oh petit mal, grand mal. I imagine my coma, my classmates' shock, mouths bright and round as finger cymbals.

Emergency room. A whirl of robes and clipboards, my parents whisked away while the nurse readies me for the electro-encephalogram. *Anyone ever pull your hair?* she asks. Her fingers warm and rough over my scalp; then the prick, sharp and soft at once, like a tack through cork. *Breathe in and out real quick, like you're scared.* She watches the skittish needle.

Her hands, neither motherly nor unmotherly, parting twists of hair. I sit still. I do what I'm told. When it's time for the electrodes to come out, she yanks them in handfuls and I feel light, faultless, thrilled.

~

Metallic chitter like a chiding kestrel, penetrating my sleep. 3 a.m. The nurse draws the curtain back and stands at my bedside, bloodwork in hand. What I've done. She wants to know exactly what I've taken. How much. Why.

I summon outrage. *Nothing, I didn't, I'm not.* My face feels bright. Her plain sneakers lend her a kind of steadfastness, while she warns, threatens, pleads. She clasps my hand, strokes the green filigree beneath skin, the fan of fine bones made visible by my clenching. Presses the intravenous needle tip, pierces, aligns its steel-mindedness with soft, slipping curves of vein.

A violet bruise spreads. The girl I don't want to be floods back through the saline drip, the bit of bloody backwash in the tube. When the nurse gets up to go I do not look at her; her image through the sac hooked to the metal stand, inverted, miniature.

# A good mother

I remember

standing at the gates of the school,
in rain, hesitant.

Often I'd be like this,
late, lost,

thinking how I'd like to be
the kind of girl

to run away; let the creek lead me along
its crooked, inky Arabic, accented

with tin cans, bottle caps, broken spokes.
To trespass,

to be queen and fighter kite,
one of those girls

behind the school, smoking, blowing clouds
of white bees; dressed

savagely, against beauty. Frayed
jeans, slashed shirts, shoplifted lipstick.

To sleep with a boy, even if it wasn't
the sweet, sparrow-eyed one –

Was this before or after the hospital?
This moment, wishing. To not

be so careful.

Like a good mother, rain
buttoned the air between sky and me.

# Tremor and flare

When I left that school, I felt like a struck bell, a single note, held in pitch, dissipating. Happy, okay, spacey.

Went to a Protestant all-girls school. Morning hymns, tennis courts, echo of an indoor pool.

Hung around with the quiet girls, learned to sing the harmonies of *Scarborough Fair Canticle*. Stepped through into the sudden common intimacy of our lives. The ones who stayed home and watched movies the evening of the father-daughter dance, the ones who dropped the invitation for the mother's Sunday brunch. The secret, bulimic lives of boarders. Stayed on the edges of their confidences. In Grade eleven, a classmate committed suicide; I attended her funeral, hadn't known her, but wanted to be there, close to it, that verdant grief of girls.

Went to the formal in Grade thirteen and wore an orchid corsage, strand of pearls, a pink bell dress with a sweetheart neckline, a silver shawl. A friend told me I looked like Natalie Wood, pleasing me.

Every now and then went to the nurse's office pretending menstrual cramps, took the Tylenol in a Dixie cup from the nurse's hand, bit into the wax as I sipped, tongued the teethmarks. Lay on the cot looking up at the ceiling. Watched the live coverage of the Challenger launch, the explosion, bewildered eyes searching the screen for signs of parachutes; watched the other girls burst into tears and wondered why I didn't feel anything. Disaster seemed flat, tiny, a shimmering tremor and flare in a blue sky.

# TELL

*R. v. Warren Paul Glowatski, 1999*

*R. v. Kelly Marie Ellard, 2000*
    *(Overturned on appeal)*

*R. v. Kelly Marie Ellard, 2004*
    *(Mistrial)*

# Examination

*Who were you when you were fifteen?*

*What could you see?*

*Were your clothes made of wool,*

*of cotton, of canvas?*

*What did you carry?*


*Do you remember the sky?*

*Do you remember the moon?*

*Do you remember the tide?*


*Did you know her?*


*Was there gravel, sand, grass?*

*Did you walk through it?*

*Was the grass wet with dew?*


*Who was your closest friend?*

*Did you walk side by side or single file?*

*Who was nearest to the road, who*

*nearest to the waterway?*

*Did you speak, or walk in silence?*


*If you reached out your arm could you touch her?*


*Did you quicken your pace? Was there*

*anything being shouted,*

*whispered?*


*How did you hurt your hand?*

*Did you take any of her possessions?*


*Did you step into the water to wash your hands*

*or did you kneel at the shoreline?*

*Were you leaving footprints on the road?*

*Mud? Sand from the soles of your shoes?*

*Clean as a whistle?*

*Had it been raining then, is that what you believe?*


*How did you travel home?*

*Was time important to you that night?*

*Were you running?*


*How long did you look back?*


*Was she facing you or the Gorge?*

*Do you know what a silhouette is?*

*Were you her protector?*


*Moonlight on the water, is that your evidence?*


*You had no anger in your heart.*

                    *(Is that a question, Counsel?)*

*You had no anger in your heart?*

*Who washed your clothes for you?*


*Who testified against you?*

# Admission of Facts

*That on the night of November 14th, 1997, there was a full moon.*
*Moonrise at 5:17 p.m., November 14th, and moonset*
*at 8:21 a.m., November 15th, 1997.*

# Satellite

*There was something in the sky –*
            *there was a weird – I don't know*
*what it was but something was happening in the sky –*

Light unfurling
in bright ribbons, braided and unbraided
across stratosphere; brighter sequins
loosened in the slipstream.
*A spaceship,*
                    *a missile.*

My mouth fell open, soft, as though I could catch
their stammer in my own.

Did she see this? I wanted someone to testify,
to ask – did she look up from her disquiet, cave
of scapula and clavicle,
so theirs became one gesture.
A field, Shoreline Middle School, the same skies
for each of them.

            *A shooting star.*

Were they like other children, then, seeing
the Russian satellite? *Red streaks going*
*across the sky,* their bodies visible

against that light. Did they feel the same. Wonder,
       or what I want
to call wonder –

           the upward tilt
       of their faces, luminous below that wake.

# Shoreline Field

What might have glistened?
Blades of grass, the glossed water
of the Gorge: dew, hoarfrost,
secret of salt, crystallized
on marsh flora.
Arrow-grass and glasswort.

*How much light?* they were asked.
In cross-examination they bristled,
knowing they'd lied, still wanting
to be believed. *It was light enough*
*that we could see. Our eyes*
*adjusted to the dark, and there was*
*the reflection of moonlight*
*from the water,*
*so we could see.*

# Craigflower Bridge, south

1.

*When the tide goes out, there's —*
*there was mud there —*

                damp of wood trestles,
the Gorge, low, *oil-black.* Tattered strands
of eelgrass. *Dingy, drab,* their feelings
no different. Nothing they wanted to touch.

Mudflats, soft and distending
under their feet. A half-circle of girls
around her, *like a horseshoe.* Then shrieks
like hot ash showering down.
*Mud, muddy, shit-*
*kicking boots. We kicked her*
*until she was curled in the mud.*

As though they hit her harder out of disgust
for tar pitch, the silvery mud,
efflorescence on the water containment wall.
     Her face, blood-
daubed, mud-daubed, *it was hard to tell.*


2.

I want to be sure      want to tell      the truth within a lie
what they withheld

the first, the lesser assault, halted

*Kelly dragged Reena down    to the water's edge*
*and kept going*

                But Kelly said it wasn't her         that she
watched from the landing     the others surround her
the rain   of hands and feet

*She's hunched     over the handrail   holding on*
*trying to haul herself    up the stairs . . .*
*They're hitting her . . .       She turns toward me*
          *and falls into me –*

                         *like this, I guess –*

In the courtroom she stands and holds out her arms –

     *and I push her back into the others*


A girl       catching another      falling
               that was all


Afterward, she crouched     by the Gorge
to wash her hands

*– Why?*

                *– Because my hands –*

3.

*I couldn't look at her,* she said

> *I walked past her*
> > *to the water's edge*

> *There was something on my hands*

> > > *I couldn't see*

> *I could feel something slimy*
> > *on my hands, between my fingers*

> > > *from when she fell into me*

# Craigflower Schoolhouse

What is given only in fragments.
Kelly turned to him, Warren said. A gaze. A grin.

*We followed her across the bridge.*

Then Kelly asked Reena
to remove her jacket, her clog boots.

What is given is an old schoolhouse, milk-washed, white
clapboard siding. A green hill. A schoolbell, iron-
tongued. – *Did Reena say anything?*      – *I don't remember.*
– *Did you? Did Kelly?*      – *I don't remember.* Green,
gossamer with dew. Clogs in the grass. A Garry
oak tree, leaves turning. – *So the assault took place*
*in silence?*      – *Words were being said but I don't remember*
*what they were.*      – *Who was saying the words?*

The way the hill shied down toward the Gorge.
Green. A bell, salvaged from a wrecked steamship.
Moon gloss on her clogs; buckles and rivets; in the creases
of her pleather jacket. What did they want? Not
for her to be on her knees; they waited, Warren said,
for her to unbend, to stand. – *When she gave up her clogs,*
*did she seem afraid?*      – *I don't remember.*      – *You can't see*
*her face?*      – *I can see her face, but it's blank to me.*

The same events given, the same withheld. A white
schoolhouse. A green hill. A toll bridge.

# Craigflower Bridge, north

*The tide was in, the tide was out, I don't know –*

Where did he stand on shore, where did
tideline lie. Where did he follow to. *I thought*
*Kelly wanted to move her to where it was*
*darker,* he said at his trial. Where was it darker,
where did moonlight, lamplight, fade. Down
the slope, their shapes blotted by the bridge's
arc and shadow. He stopped, he said.
Where? Where shoreline began. Reena
suddenly roused by the touch of cold,
so that she came to her feet in the water
to struggle again with Kelly.

– *I had sand on my shoes.*     – *Didn't you say*
*your shoes were wet, muddy? You were in the water.*
– *I was at the water's edge. I was on the sand.*
White jeans splattered to mid-calf, to knees.
Blotches of water. Caked sand, clotted mud.
Where did grass give way to gravel. – *I stood*
*on the shore,* he insisted. *There was grass*
*all the way down from the road. My shoes*
*were wet from the dew in the grass,*
*sir. I stood on the shore.*

# Satellite (Mistrial)

– *I leaned*

        *over the bridge,*

              said Kelly.

*I was waiting.*

*I leaned on my elbows*

        *and looked over the water.*

      *I was dazed, yes.*

              – *And it's dark out,*

                  *obviously?*

– *Yes, but the light* –

           – *But it was a clear, starry night?*

    – *I – I can't remember.*

              – *A full moon that night?*

– *I can't remember.*

        – *You can't remember. There was a satellite*
      *earlier that night in the sky. Can you recall that?*

*– Yes, I remember the – I believe it was*
*a meteor shower, not a satellite,*

        *but I don't recall a full moon, no. I could have*
          *seen it, but I don't remember.*

Her testimony

        dazzling

   moon,

          stars,

     satellite,

the bridge,

        rage

# Clean

*I have*
*a white floor*
*and the floor was clean,*
*there wasn't any mud on it,*

said Kelly's stepmother, testifying
in her daughter's defense.

Cool linoleum.

The Gorge by Craigflower Bridge,
full
of *seaweed and filth and mud,*

her daughter's skin

clean, white.

# Inland waters

Rivers I knew as unravellings of light, as we drove over bridges. As unfolding scraps of colour. Tin roofs, speckled chickens, turmeric-stained grindstones. Rivers that flowed on in the names of their surroundings. *Rivière Terre-Rouge, Rivière des Anguilles, des Citronniers, des Galets, Rivière Tabac, Rivière Sèche . . .* Culverted rivers, drained swamps, on an island once rich in marshlands. Dodo bones drowsing in the soft mud of Mare-aux-Songes.

Boom irrigators in the sugar cane fields: mist and steel skeleton. The disowned strangeness of reservoirs where we skipped stones and slammed our voices into the air to hear the echo; hum of electrical towers like the onset of deafness. Still water, a feeling held in.

White salt, black basalt tiles at the salterns at the Gorges de la Rivière Noire. Women in wide-brimmed hats leaning over pyramids of salt, harvesting by hand the grey grains of *fleur-de-sel*. Weather threatening. Chemistry changed by the slightest rainfall. And if it rained, then, donning rubber boots, shovelling it all away, sluicing the pools clean.

# See them say

Mistrials,
overturned verdicts.
Transcripts of earlier testimony
placed before the witness,
past and present overlaid
like vellum, the defence
cross-examining each
falsehood, each fault or failure
of memory. *I was tricked,* said one.

On the stand they were always
thirteen, fourteen, fifteen.
The boy who was Warren's friend,
diagnosed with post-traumatic stress
disorder; the girl who testified
to seeing Kelly and Warren
cross the bridge together,
dead at seventeen, *heart failure.*
Then she was only a recording,
a click, a lick of ribbon,
a hiss of white noise.

*Voir-dire.* See, say,
to see them say, say
what is true. Warren said
he and Kelly made a pact,

that he'd say he beat up a Native
for calling her a hootchie.
The year he recanted he traced
Métis lines in his cheekbones,
asked to be transferred
to Kwikwèxwelhp Healing Village.

*I remind you, witness,*
*that you are ſtill under oath.*
Offered a glass of water
when they wept. They drank
without thirst, without lowering their eyes.

Kelly shouted in the courtroom
at the prosecutor:
*– You can say anything you want*
*but everything that comes out of your mouth*
*is going to be wrong.*

> *– What did you say?* asked the Crown.

*– What is coming out of your mouth –*

*what you are saying –*
> *everything that comes out of*
>> *your mouth –*

# THE LANDSCAPE WITHOUT HER

*What's more important? The beginning*
*or the end? That they went*
*or that they returned? And what is over?*
                                    *– Tracy K. Smith*

*R. v. Kelly Marie Ellard (2005)*
    *(Appealed; conviction restored in 2009)*

# Tillicum Bridge

On the underside of Tillicum
I turn my back to the water

        lace fingers through chain-link
           to look at stone

where they found

        *fire-altered rock, ash and charcoal . . .*
           *shell remains from oysters,*
               *mussels, clams and crabs . . .*

(a fence around natural stone
           as though stone might turn feral)

Four thousand years old

*. . . the bones of fish, deer and seals . . .*
        *fragments left*
           *from the making of stone tools . . .*

Middens, tells, the archaeologist said

        (*tell*, a word from Arabic, from Hebrew

a site that holds evidence
           of successive human occupation

to untell, to uncover the layers
    of this evidence

                                        to retell, to try to restore the site
                                to its original state)


... *herring, salmon, a variety of birds* ...

            Each site an event
                        destroyed by the process
                                    through which we read it

            broken strata
                                    ruined interrelation of artifacts

                *site loss*

Still we read
                        *red, oxidized earth*
                                    *scorched rock, fire-cracked rock*


            the wrecking-ball wisdom of archaeology

things can only be uncovered
                                                once

# Admission of Facts

*And lastly,*
*that the identity, continuity and integrity of the body of Reena Virk*
*are admitted for all purposes.*

# Craigflower Bridge

*Get up.*

A bridge is wood trestle below, metal
above; a guardrail

of teal-green lattice. Hennaed patches of rust.
"I need help. I need help. I need help."

A bridge is a distance, measured in steps, in pools
of lamplight, the time it takes to cross.

In breaths. – *How far did you watch her go?*
– *Halfway across, to where the light spreads out.*

Headlights of passing cars, bright beads on a wire
that curves into darkness: Highway 1A, Gorge Road.

– *Did you observe her gait as she crossed?*
I thought of the gaits of Indian dance,

the little I learned, carrying
my clumsiness far into adulthood:

elephant, peacock, deer. – *She was
staggering, light-headed.*

A bridge is held up by belief that you will go
over to the other shore

to someone who wants you, to somewhere
safe.

# Lovely, alive

At a distance, it could be
dancing,

the way I danced,
flinging my limbs out
for the tug of rib cage, the snag
at centre. Could be drunkenness, my hand
on an oak banister in a Forest Hill home, boozy
sashay of crushed velvet at my knees. My friend's face
hazy, laughing. Lovely. Clove cigarettes
alive with tangerine coils and crackles, each drag
leaving cinnamon on our tongues.

Could be the rocking
of subway cars, the engined tow. Morning, I watched
her eyes, the fast, jittery movement of her gaze,
gemmed, blue-green, as signs and stations
veered away from us.

I want to tell you about being sixteen, seventeen,
travelling with my dad to an island
off the coast of Venezuela,
diving coral reefs,
fish blossoming in my hand,
angel, damsel, butterfly.
Boom of breath against eardrum.

Hollow pop and pennywhistle of my father's
underwater camera, a sound
so wild it was far and interior at once.
I held onto the slides for a long time. Never showed them
to anyone.
Glass-masked, ribbed tube between lips and gums,
finned feet, I was not grace. But I could

live with it, the argument
with a lesser gravity, the dangle
        of arms and legs,
gawky, undulant, tangled in sunlight.

# Narrows

The woman who walks with me knows the uses
of each plant, each separate part: leaf,
flower and fruit; bulb and root,
heartwood.
     All morning
we lean into the banks of the Gorge,

November light, greeny-gold,
her brown skin sheened, hair fanned and sun-fired
over the neck of her Cowichan sweater. I ask her
to tell me the names of trees,
by the bridge, the schoolhouse, down to shoreline,
ones they examined as though to harvest *strands of hair,*
*reddish material,* hands moving over smooth or rough bark.

Her name is Cheryl. She gives me names
and more; what plants for nourishment, for medicine;
for thread and rope, for dyes; for the adornment
of the body. *This we used in ceremonies for the dead –*
     she drops her eyes – *I can't tell you*
*more than that. This we used for yellow; this we used for red.*

Yes, she says, she followed the trials, thinking of the children
in her family, her sister, herself
when she was young. *I grew up in this skin.*
Sinewy-limbed arbutus,
        its lavish shedding,
    red bark peeling in shattered scrolls.

~

*There was a white piece of wood –*
> *Kelly said she'd messed up her face with a stick,*
> *a white stick, a – I don't know*

> *what it's called – and hit her, or –*
*– cut her – I can't remember exactly – but I know*
> *that she hurt Reena's face with it –*

> But no other testimony to this,

not even Warren's, nor the pathologist's. Only
the field identification officer who walked the tideline
until he found *a white stake.*

Seafoam, willow leaves, gull feathers; eelgrass
and tossed cigarettes. Bits of testimony stranded. The girl's
recollection, its wild
specificity –

> *A white piece of wood like what surveyors –*
> > *surveyors use to – like –*
> *mark boundaries or whatever –*

~

The girl crying on the banks said,
*My father is angry with me and won't give me*
*anything to eat.*

Her name was Camosun. The spirit who heard her
gave her sturgeon, but she said, *Naw, I don't like that.*
So he threw it east to the mainland river.
He gave her cranberries, but she said,
*Naw, I don't like that either.* So he threw them
to the westward lake.
                    She refused many things,
but duck, herring, coho and oyster
she accepted,
and this is why these are plentiful in the Gorge.

*Naw.* Mouthy. She wants
what she wants: shakes her head, full-
cheeked, smear of fish oil, salty and shining
on her lips. Crush of herring eggs beneath her tongue.
How entangled they are, hunger and greed.

Cheryl offers her story, laughing. She doesn't need
to be grieved, this girl, even as she is turned

to stone, her people to trees that would *clutch the sky.*

~

What did we miss?

We go back through testimony, wanting something
sure, something to shore up the verdict.

The banks once lush
with blue camas, chocolate lily, white fawn lily.

Water taken from the Gorge,
its salinity, its mineral composition

held against *white crystalline material* ringing a girl's jacket.

*. . . serpentine residue*
       *along the waist,*
            *the cuffs of both sleeves . . .*


~


*Do you want to see her?* Cheryl asks me.

We drive further south to Tillicum's arch
       over the Gorge Narrows.

Through here, the current quickens,
water silken,

sucked down into swirls. *Soie gorge-de-pigeon,*
       shot silk, dusky, iridescent.

Old typewritten text, taloned letters, a crooked *a*,
clutching the sheet of paper, describing Camosun's shape:

moss-dark rock, barely visible beneath.

Inland waters emptying towards the sea,
            seawater forcing its way against the river
      as the tide rises. The myth

of how the Songhees dove, touched the stone body below,

washed their garments in the shining whorl
*to protect their wearers from drowning.*

Cheryl says nothing. *Avoir la gorge serrée*, to be close to tears.

# Life in these waters

The argument, years ago, over the diver's observation
that *the body looked untouched by nature.*

> *Certainly you're not saying there's no life in these waters?*

If you could say what life there is. Say sea tar lichen. Say snails,
barnacles, periwinkles. Oysters and blue mussels. Little neck
and butter clams. Say urchin, kelp, green and red algae.

Say cormorant. Glaucous-winged gull, green-winged teal, blue
heron. Say stickleback, sculpin, bullhead; coho salmon, chum
salmon, herring and cutthroat trout. Otter's lithe body, sharp
teeth, animal curiosity. Would it have been an indignity,
to say this?

Even there, where the mudflats had been rich. Say parchment
worms, ghost and mud shrimp, soft-shelled clams. Green
burrowing anemone.

Say it now. Say eelgrass meadow. Shore crab, sand dollar, say
brittle star, mottled sea star, ochre sea star. Say moon snail,
blood star. Her body. *Eelgrass was the only life I observed.*

# Curfew

*Was time important to you that night?*
Yes, they said.

*Did you abide by a curfew?* Ten o'clock,
eleven, midnight.

*Who greeted you?* Mothers who kissed
their daughters goodnight, mothers who checked
their daughters' breath.

*Who greeted you?* No mothers; girls signed their names
in the register, and women who were not their mothers
initialed the time.

*How long did it last?* A moment.

How long is a moment?

*How long did it last?* the Crown asked Warren.
*– I don't know. – How long did it feel like? – Forever.*

*How long does it take to walk across the bridge?*

*How long does it take to walk home?*

*I'm fucked, I'm fucked for the rest of my life.* Warren,

overheard crying to his father, the night of his arrest.
The tidal chart entered as an exhibit, indicating *the time lapse between high waters and low waters.*

*I don't remember. It was so long ago,* Kelly repeated,
a monotone. Her second trial. At her third, she fell silent.

How old the Gorge, how old the middens. *All carbon-14 dates have probability errors, as atmospheric testing of nuclear weapons changed radiocarbon amounts in the natural world.*

How long the trials. Twelve years.

*How long did you look back?*
I remember

being fifteen, lying on my best friend's bed, listening
to *Forever Young* by Alphaville. How badly I wanted a boy
to slow dance that song with.

# Her throat

Her throat was thick, mannish;
muscled, tendoned, burl
        of Adam's apple beneath

burnished skin.

What pools in the hollow at the base
is want. It flared

in the rumours of her –
giving the boys head,
stealing a girl's phone book
to call the numbers, fling out lies like salt, so they would

see her.

She stepped out that night wanting
forgiveness, a sleepover;
stuffed her pyjamas and diary in her bag;
took the bus to the Towne & Country mall
to meet them. Wanted to lay down her confidences

on her friend's shoulder, that space below clavicle,
cool, smooth,
impervious earth below stone.

Her face, down-shadowed
from upper lip, chin, to soft underside.
All the tremors of
            words, swallows, inhalation,
giving her away. How she
wanted to be chosen –

hirsute, dark – as she was.

# Chandlo

If I could
slow it down. I trace
a finger on my forehead, the feel

of it, like the bright red dot
my grandmothers, my great-aunts wore.
A gesture learned in girlhood: smudge

of vermilion,
        kumkum, sandalwood paste.
    Saffron and kusumba flower.

Crushed ash and scorn. If I could salve it.
*When a woman adorns herself*
*with a bindi, she adds*

                *the grace of four moons*
*to her face.* Tilak bindi, tear-shaped,
chandlo bindi, moon-shaped. If I could

    turn to see it,
the white girl's hand, the cigarette, the twist:
    the blistered moment

           before Reena's hands flew up,
the moment she faced
    her beholders, a seared moon between her eyes.

# Enough

Grace is the girl who cradles her knuckles, the uttered cuss,
the upper cut

against teeth

grass stains, streaks of green on a boy's jeans, he who
delivered punting kicks to the head

until his best friend jerked him away, pushed him
down against the hill

Grace is the hierarchy of girlhood that lets some girls reign, lets
one of them say, *She's had enough*

Grace is breath returning, and with it, spasms of pain,
the seine of it, tightening against torso

Glimmer above, stars or rivets, she can't be sure. Rivulets of
moonlight below, in mud

Murmur of cars passing overhead. Grace is knees, hands and
knees, knees and hillside

She said, "Help me. I love you." One girl wept while her boyfriend
held her

Grace is enough, cruelty casual enough it can be called to an end
like that

# To tear with the teeth

*– The tide was in, the tide was out, I don't know –*
*– Why did you tell a lie about the tide?*

The sky today, the same faded blue
as my mother's nikkah sari. Clouds like tarnished sequins.
I want to lay down flowers, but it feels intrusive;
instead I walk across the bridge and count my steps.
Downstream, a cormorant dives; I follow it
in mind, a pendant yanked, bubbles a strand of pearls
loosened and scattered. *Gorgeous,* from the Old French
for throat, for a stone that adorns the throat.

　　　　If something is allowed to flood and recede
and flood again. Twelve years of trials. A childhood.
Notebooks filled with my anxious cursive, *I* like a fishhook
on each line. Why is it so hard
to say it? Guidebooks, passages underlined. *If you run a strand*
*of eelgrass through the teeth, it makes a sound like 'hsh.'*
Heisha-heisha, meaning, *to tear with the teeth.*
*It's like it wants to be hushed,* Cheryl said.

Halocline: the deeper body of seawater, blue-green,
moving upstream; glassine freshwater flowing down.
In another time it would have been possible to see this:
two waters.  The Gorge in its abundance. Meadows of eelgrass.
Algae like drifts of organza, green and reddish bronze. I watch

as a heron stilt-walks in sunlight, spreads blue-grey wings
casting shadows on the water that diminish the glare, show the fish
beneath the surface.

# NOTICE TO THE READER

Reena Virk was a girl of South Asian descent who was murdered on November 14th, 1997, in Saanich, British Columbia. At least eight young people participated in the initial assault on the south side of Craigflower Bridge, while more looked on. Seven of her assailants were girls; five were white. Among them were Kelly Ellard and Warren Glowatski.

Virk rose from that beating and walked north across the bridge toward home. Her drowned body was found in the Gorge Waterway.

Glowatski was tried and convicted of second-degree murder in 1999. Ellard underwent three trials for the same offence. She was convicted in 2000, and appealed; her second trial in 2004 ended in a hung jury; in 2005 she was convicted again and again appealed. The Supreme Court of Canada reinstated her conviction in 2009. Ellard has steadfastly maintained her innocence.

Italicized text in these poems is mostly derived from the transcripts of the trials of Glowatski and Ellard, and my notes from attendance, when time permitted, at the 2004 and 2005 trials. In some instances text has been collaged from multiple answers within the same line of questioning, with care not to distort meaning. The testimony may or may not be true; I have cited statements that were contested, contradicted, and in some cases recanted.

Glowatski pled not guilty at his trial, but ultimately admitted complicity, testifying against Ellard at her trial in 2004. Ellard denied ever crossing the bridge, and through her defence counsel challenged the testimony containing any allegations against her; the court did not rule on the truth of each of such allegations. In the absence of physical evidence linking Ellard to the crime, apart from the strongly suggestive evidence of salt lines on the jacket Ellard wore that night, the Crown relied on Glowatski's testimony and that of peers to whom Ellard allegedly bragged about beating and drowning Virk. The defence challenged this by arguing that witnesses lied to protect themselves or each other, or that their memories had been tainted by rumours in the days following Virk's murder.

# NOTES

Craigflower Bridge was originally built in 1853 to provide settler children access to the Old Craigflower Schoolhouse, now a designated heritage site. A shell midden in the area of the Schoolhouse dates back 2,700 years.

Tillicum Bridge is further south along the Waterway: test excavations provided evidence that Native peoples lived at this location over 4,000 years ago, making this the oldest known archaeological site on southern Vancouver Island. The narrowing of the land created reversing waterfalls or whirlpools which were essential both to tidal life and the Songhee myth of Camosun. The area was dynamited in the 1960s to make passage for pleasure boats.

The text in 'Tillicum Bridge' is taken in part from signs by the bridge and correspondence with Grant Keddie, Curator of Archaeology at the Royal BC Museum.

The myth of Camosun is as told by Cheryl Bryce, Songhees First Nation of the Lekwungen ancestral land.

The reference to carbon-14 dating in 'Curfew' is taken from *Victoria Underfoot: Excavating a City's Secrets*, edited by Brenda Clark, Nicole Kilburn and Nick Russell (Madeira Park: Harbour Publishing, 2008).

The proverb in 'Chandlo' is cited in *The Grace of Four Moons: Dress, Adornment, and the Art of the Body in Modern India* by Pravina Shukla (Bloomington: Indiana University Press, 2008).

The information on eelgrass in 'To tear with the teeth' relates to the Nuu-chah-nulth origin of the name of Hesquiat, and is cited in *Botanica North America: The Illustrated Guide to Our Native Plants, Their Botany, History, and the Way They Have Shaped Our World* by Marjorie Harris (New York: HarperCollins Publishers Inc., 2003).

Accounts that Reena said "Help me, I love you" were described in a magazine feature, "Girls kill teenage schoolmate," by Patricia Chisholm (*Maclean's*, December 8, 1997).

The poem 'Craigflower Bridge' was inspired by Natasha Bakht's choreography, *Bridges* (2012), and the poem by Lynda Collins published in the accompanying program.

# ACKNOWLEDGEMENTS

I am grateful for the support of the Canada Council for the Arts, the Ontario Arts Council and the Toronto Arts Council in the research and writing of this work. The purchase of transcripts was made possible by grants through the OAC Writer's Reserve from *Arc*, *Brick Books* and *The New Quarterly*; my thanks to the editors of these publications.

Deepest thanks to Sheila Batacharya for her friendship and her tireless work on the case of Reena Virk and the well-being of girls and women of colour. I am indebted to the fearless and compassionate writing that is contained in *Reena Virk: Critical Perspectives on a Canadian Murder*, edited by Mythili Rajiva and Sheila Batacharya.

To Kim Jernigan for taking notice of some of these poems and publishing them in *The New Quarterly* alongside the writings of women I have great respect for: Heather Spears, author of *Required Reading: A witness in words and drawings to the Reena Virk Trials 1998–2000*, and Joan MacLeod, author of *The Shape of a Girl*. Thank you to Sarah Selecky for featuring a series of poems on her blog.

To Cheryl Bryce, Songhees First Nation of the Lekwungen ancestral land, for sharing her knowledge of the profound work on the cultural and ecological restoration that she has led along the Gorge Waterway. Likewise to Grant Keddie, Curator of Archaeology at the Royal BC Museum, for his correspondence.

To the faculty and graduates of the Creative Writing MFA program at the University of Guelph, including Constance Rooke, whom

I was honoured to meet; Ken Babstock and my fellow students in the poetry workshop; my thesis supervisor, Janice Kulyk Keefer, and my mentor for the summer term, Tim Lilburn.

For his continuing mentorship and 'delight, the pleasure' of his company, Gerry Shikatani. For holding witnessing and practice at the heart, Suzanne Robertson. Without you both, this work would not have come to fruition.

For their generous responses to this project in its early stages: George Elliott Clarke, as well as John Steffler and the participants of the Sage Hill Poetry Colloquium. For friendship and innumerable exchanges on living and writing: Anna Chatterton, Evalyn Parry, Guy Ewing, Gitanjali Kolanad and Karin Randoja. Ronna Bloom, for a room where my attention shifted from her wild socks to her grave face.

Hélène, for being there.

For sustaining me with love and belief, all these years, dearest Mark. For my daughter (*Ah, cette fille, elle est éveillée!*). Mes parents et mes frères.

Karine Guyon, for lending us her powerful image; and Beth Oberholtzer, for her exquisite design. Infinite gratitude and respect to Beth Follett who encouraged me to draw deeper still from the well.